The
CRADLE,
CROSS,
and
CROWN

BILLY GRAHAM

THOMAS NELSON
Since 1798

Published in Nashville, Tennessee, by Thomas Nelson.

Portions of this book were excerpted from *This Christmas Night* by Billy and Ruth Graham © 2007, and from *Hope for Each Day* by Billy Graham © 2002. Used by permission.

Thomas Nelson titles may be purchased in bulk for educational, business, fund-raising, or sales promotional use. For information, please e-mail SpecialMarkets@ThomasNelson.com.

Scripture quotations are taken from The Holy Bible, New International Version®, NIV®. Copyright © 1973, 1978, 1984, 2011 by Biblica, Inc.® Used by permission of Zondervan. All rights reserved worldwide. www.Zondervan.com. The "NIV" and "New International Version" are trademarks registered in the United States Patent and Trademark Office by Biblica, Inc.®

Scripture quotations marked NKJV are taken from the New King James Version®. Copyright © 1982 by Thomas Nelson. Used by permission. All rights reserved. Scripture quotations marked PHILLIPS are from J. B. Phillips: THE NEW TESTAMENT IN MODERN ENGLISH, 1962 edition by Harper Collins.

ISBN 13: 978-0-529-10498-4

Printed in the United States

20 21 22 POLL 11 10 9

www.thomasnelson.com

Foreword

....

In the midst of all the upheaval and crisis and difficulty and problems and fear, comes the message of Christmas with all of its hope, goodwill, and cheer. I think the message of Christmas has been terribly misapplied and misunderstood for many years in this country. Some think of business profits, shopping, gifts, tinsel, toys, and celebration. Others think only of Bethlehem, of the star in the sky, shepherds in the field and angels singing. Still others cynically ask, "Where is this Prince of Peace in a world filled with so much trouble?"

The real Christmas message goes far deeper. It heralds the entrance of God into human history. It is heaven descending to earth. It is as though a trumpeter had taken his stand upon the turrets of time and announced to a despairing, hopeless, and frustrated world the coming of the Prince of Peace. It answers all the great questions that plague the human race at this hour. The Christmas message is relevant, revolutionary, and reassuring to us today. I believe it can be summed up in three words: a cradle, a Cross, and a crown.

The
CRADLE

God Visited Earth

....

O n that first Christmas night the Bible tells us about the angel coming to those fearful shepherds and saying, "Fear not, I bring you good news." What is the real meaning of that good news?

During World War II, many a mother would take her son and try to keep the memory of the father who was away at war in the memory of that boy. And one mother I heard about took her son every day into the bedroom and showed him a large portrait of the father who was away. One day the little boy said to his mother, "Mom, wouldn't it be great if Dad could just step out of the frame?"

That's what happened that first Christmas. For centuries man has looked into the heavens longing for God to step out of the frame, and at Bethlehem that's exactly what God did. Incredible and unbelievable as it may appear to a modern man, the Bible teaches that Jesus Christ was a visitor from Heaven itself. He was God Incarnate.

> And there were shepherds living out in the fields nearby, keeping watch over their flocks at night. An angel of the Lord appeared to them, and the glory of the Lord shone around them, and they were terrified. But the angel said to them, "Do not be afraid. I bring you good news that will cause great joy for all the people. Today in the town of David a Savior has been born to you; he is the Messiah, the Lord. This will be a sign to you: You will find a baby wrapped in cloths and lying in a manger."
>
> —LUKE 2:8–12

No Ordinary Sheep

Those were no ordinary sheep . . .
no common flocks,
huddled in sleep
among the fields,
the layered rocks,
near Bethlehem
That Night;
but those
selected for the Temple sacrifice:
theirs to atone
for sins
they had not done.
How right
the angels should appear
to them

That Night.
Those were no usual shepherds there,
but outcast shepherds
whose unusual care
of special sheep
made it impossible to keep
Rabbinic law,
which therefore banned them.
How right
the angels should appear
to them
That Night.

—Ruth Bell Graham's *Collected Poems*

A tiny secluded manger, with its sweet-smelling straw and its lowing cattle, comprised the homely stage upon which the most striking and significant drama of the centuries was enacted. It was there that God, in the Person of His Son, Jesus Christ, became identified with man. In meekness and humility He came to earth as the Prince of Peace.

—This Christmas Night

Christmas is a time of miracles. The angelic chorus, lowly shepherds, a humble manger as the birthplace of deity—all are miraculous happenings.

—KENNETH W. OSBECK

Away in a Manger

....

Away in a manger,
no crib for a bed,
the little Lord Jesus
laid down His sweet head;
the stars in the sky
looked down where He lay,
the little Lord Jesus,
asleep on the hay.

The cattle are lowing;
the Baby awakes,
but little Lord Jesus,
no crying He makes;
I love Thee, Lord Jesus!
look down from the sky,
and stay by my cradle
till morning is nigh.

Be near me, Lord Jesus,
I ask Thee to stay
close by me forever,
and love me, I pray;
bless all the dear children
in Thy tender care,
and fit us for heaven,
to live with Thee there.

—John Thomas McFarland, 1851–1913

Eternal Impact

....

The virgin-born baby was God in human form. He humbled Himself, He took the form of a servant, He was made in your likeness and mine, He identified Himself with the problems of the human race. And thus it was that the apostle John wrote, "The Word was made flesh, and dwelt among us, (and we beheld His glory, as of the only begotten of the Father.)" (John 1:14 KJV).

In the early days of the nineteenth century, the world was following, with fear and trembling, the march of Napoleon across Europe. Day after day they waited with impatience for the latest news of the wars. And no one was paying any attention to the babies that were being born. In just one year, lying midway between Trafalgar and Waterloo, there came into the world a host of heroes. During that year of 1809, listen to the people who were born in that year—when everybody was taken up with the problems of Napoleon: Gladstone was born in Liverpool, England; Alfred Tennyson was born in Somersby, England; Oliver Wendell Holmes was born in Cambridge, Massachusetts; Frederic Chopin was born in Warsaw, Poland; Mendelssohn was born in Hamburg, Germany; and Abraham Lincoln was born in Hodgenville, Kentucky. But nobody thought of babies. Everybody was thinking of battles.

Yet over two hundred years later, with a truer perspective which the years enable us to command, we can ask ourselves, "Which of the battles of 1809 were more important than the babies of 1809?"

In the beginning was the Word, and the Word was with God, and the Word was God. He was with God in the beginning. Through him all things were made; without him nothing was made that has been made. In him was life, and that life was the light of all mankind. The light shines in the darkness, and the darkness has not overcome it.

—JOHN 1:1-5

What a difference the baby born in Bethlehem's manger two thousand years ago makes to our world today. The educational systems He has inspired, the social reforms that His teachings have instituted, and the transformation of families and lives that have come about as a result of a baby born at Bethlehem! The whole world was thinking of Caesar. The whole world was thinking of Rome. But in God's eternal plan, He was thinking of a baby in a manger in the little tiny town of Bethlehem.

Christmas is not a myth, not
a tradition, not a dream—
it is a glorious reality.

—*This Christmas Night*

Have you ever thought about what has happened because Christ came into the world? That baby in the manger of Bethlehem grew up to become our crucified and risen Savior—and the world has never been the same.

Jesus' compassion has made the world more compassionate. His healing touch has made the world more humanitarian. His self-lessness has made the world more self-effacing. Christ drew a rainbow of hope around the shoulders of men and women and gave them something to live for.

If Christ had not come, our world would indeed be a hopeless world. If Christ had not come, ours would be a lost world. There would be no access to God, there would be no atonement for sin, there would be no forgiveness, and there would be no Savior.

Yes, Christ came into the world and made it a better place. And He will do the same for you if you will open your life to Him.

—Hope for Each Day

Once in Royal David's City

Once in royal David's city
Stood a lowly cattle shed,
Where a mother laid her Baby
In a manger for His bed:
Mary was that mother mild,
Jesus Christ her little Child.

He came down to earth from heaven,
Who is God and Lord of all,
And His shelter was a stable,
And His cradle was a stall;
With the poor, and mean, and lowly,
Lived on earth our Savior holy.

And our eyes at last shall see Him,
Through His own redeeming love;
For that Child so dear and gentle
Is our Lord in heaven above,
And He leads His children on
To the place where He is gone.

—Cecil Francis Alexander, 1848

Christ came into this world as
God's Ambassador, sent from
heaven to tell us of God's love.

—*THIS CHRISTMAS NIGHT*

So they hurried off and found Mary and Joseph, and the baby, who was lying in the manger. When they had seen him, they spread the word concerning what had been told them about this child, and all who heard it were amazed at what the shepherds said to them. But Mary treasured up all these things and pondered them in her heart. The shepherds returned, glorifying and praising God for all the things they had heard and seen, which were just as they had been told.

—LUKE 2:16–20

May the Christmas morning make
us happy to be Thy children,
and the Christmas evening bring
us to our beds with grateful
thoughts, forgiving and forgiven.

—ROBERT LOUIS STEVENSON

The
CROSS

The Greetest Transformer

....

F or Christmas to have meaning, it cannot be separated from the Cross. The angel said at the birth of Jesus, "He shall save his people from their sins" (Matthew 1:21 KJV). Jesus Himself said, speaking of His death, "To this end was I born" (John 18:37 KJV). He was the only person that's ever been born in history who was born with the purpose of dying. The apostle Paul years later said, "Christ Jesus came into the world to save sinners."

The central message of Christmas is that Jesus Christ, by His death and resurrection, can transform both individuals and society. Almost everyone at some time or another feels moral guilt and failure. It's like the little boy who said, "I guess I was born wrong." In every newspaper or magazine that we pick up, and in every news-cast that we watch, we see a picture of hate and lust and greed and prejudice and corruption manifested in a thousand ways. And the fact that we have policemen and jails and military forces indicates that something is wrong with the human race, something's radically wrong with human nature.

Have the same mindset as Christ Jesus: Who, being in very nature God, did not consider equality with God something to be used to his own advantage; rather, he made himself nothing by taking the very nature of a servant, being made in human likeness. And being found in appearance as a man, he humbled himself by becoming obedient to death—even death on a cross!

—PHILIPPIANS 2:5–8

Man—A Paradox

....

Every time I board an airplane they search my luggage, and they even search my clothes on some occasions. And we ask ourselves, "What's wrong? Why can't we solve our problems? Why can't the world find this peace that this Prince of Peace was supposed to bring?" You see, man is actually a paradox. On the one hand there's futility and sin, on the other there's goodness and kindness and gentleness and love. On the one hand he's a moral failure, and on the other hand he has the capacities that would relate him to Almighty God. No wonder the apostle Paul called this moral failure "the mystery of iniquity" (2 Thessalonians 2:7 KJV).

The Bible teaches that the human race is morally sick. This disease has affected every phase of our life in society. The Bible calls this disease by an ugly, three-letter word: sin.

He was despised and rejected by
   mankind,
a man of suffering, and familiar
   with pain.
Like one from whom people hide
   their faces
he was despised, and we held him
   in low esteem.

Surely he took up our pain
and bore our suffering, yet we
   considered him punished by God,
stricken by him, and afflicted.
But he was pierced for our
   transgressions,
he was crushed for our iniquities;
the punishment that brought us
   peace was on him,
and by his wounds we are healed.

—Isaiah 53:3–5

The Only Cure for Sin

....

T he Bible teaches that the only cure for sin is the blood of Christ on that Cross. Every Protestant, Catholic, and Orthodox church celebrates Communion. When we put the wine to our lips, it's the symbol of that blood that was shed. And one of the most prominent aspects of the worship of ancient Judaism was the shedding of blood to make an atonement for sin. The word *blood* symbolizes life, a life that was given. Christ became the Lamb of God whose blood was shed, and He died on the Cross for our sins.

The Cross and the resurrection stand today as humanity's only hope. It was on Good Friday and Easter that God did for us what we could not do for ourselves. From these momentous events, God is saying to sinful man, "I love you. I love you so much I gave My Son." But He's saying more than that. He's saying, "I can for-give you, because of what He did on the Cross." And this is good news at this Christmas!

They had seen an angel, they repeated. And the angel had told them about a Baby born in Bethlehem and called the Baby "Savior" and "Lord." They had just seen the Baby with their own eyes—out in the stable behind the inn—and they wanted everyone else to know about it too.

He was a tiny thing, wrapped tightly in a long linen band of cloth and sleeping soundly as any newborn baby. Sleeping as though the world had not waited thousands of years for this moment. As soundly as though your life and my life and the lives of everyone on earth were not wrapped up in His birth.

—Our Christmas Story, *This Christmas Night*

Free from the Law

Free from the law, O happy condition,
Jesus hath bled, and there is remission;
Cursed by the law and bruised by the fall,
Grace hath redeemed us once for all.

Once for all, O sinner, receive it,
Once for all, O brother, believe it;
Cling to the cross, the burden will fall,
Christ hath redeemed us once for all.

Now we are free, there's no condemnation,
Jesus provides a perfect salvation;
"Come unto Me," O hear His sweet call,
Come, and He saves us once for all.

Once for all, O sinner, receive it,
Once for all, O brother, believe it;
Cling to the cross, the burden will fall,
Christ hath redeemed us once for all.

"Children of God," O glorious calling,
Surely His grace will keep us from falling;
Passing from death to life at His call,
Blessed salvation once for all.

Once for all, O sinner, receive it,
Once for all, O brother, believe it;
Cling to the cross, the burden will fall,
Christ hath redeemed us once for all.

—Philip Paul Bliss, 1838–1876

We Must Do Our Part

....

G od did His part by giving His Son, the
great Christmas gift, God's great gift to
the human race. But we must do something.
We must humble ourselves. We must admit our
sins. We must admit that we're moral failures
and turn to Him by faith. We must say as the
publican did, "God, have mercy on me, a sinner"
(Luke 18:13). The Scripture says that a bro-
ken and a contrite heart God will not despise
(Psalm 34:18). If we as individuals and as a
nation would humble ourselves and turn from
our sins, God has promised forgiveness, healing
to the nation, and eternal life to the individual
(2 Chronicles 7:14).

This is the good news that the world is mor-
ally, psychologically, and spiritually longing for.
Some of you may dismiss it as idiotic and ridic-
ulous that a man dying 2,000 years ago could

be relevant today. The apostle Paul anticipated we'd say that when he said, "The preaching of the cross is, I know, nonsense to those who are involved in this dying world. But to us who are being saved from that death, it's nothing less than the power of God" (1 Corinthians 1:18 PHILLIPS).

Our Greatest Need

....

I believe that America and the world stand on the threshold of divine judgment. Morally, socially, economically, politically, spiritually, we are in deep trouble. We've turned away from God, and every month seems to take us further away from the only One who can reverse the tide, forgive our sins, and forestall the imminent judgment. We must alter our course if we are going to see many more Christmas seasons. We must reorder our priorities. We must remake the unjust structures that have taken advantage of the powerless, and broken the hearts of the poor and the dispossessed. We all admit that we need more sweeping social reform, and in true repentance we must determine to do something about it.

But even that, as good as it is, is not our greatest need. Our greatest need is a change in our hearts. That is why Jesus said, "You must be born again" (John 3:7). That's why He said, "Unless you repent, you will all likewise perish" (Luke 13:3 NKJV). The apostle Paul in his famous sermon at Mars Hill said, "God . . . commands all men everywhere to repent, because He has appointed a day on which He will judge the world"(Acts 17:30–31 NKJV). Who should repent? Everybody. This is what the Cross calls for. The heart of its message is simple: repent and be saved—now and eternally.

Christmas is a reminder from God Himself that we are not alone.

—THIS CHRISTMAS NIGHT

O Come, O Come, Emmanuel

....

O come, O come, Emmanuel
And ransom captive Israel
That mourns in lonely exile here
Until the Son of God appear
Rejoice! Rejoice! Emmanuel
Shall come to thee, O Israel.

O come, Thou Rod of Jesse, free
Thine own from Satan's tyranny
From depths of Hell Thy people save
And give them victory o'er the grave
Rejoice! Rejoice! Emmanuel
Shall come to thee, O Israel.

O come, Thou Day-Spring, come and cheer
Our spirits by Thine advent here

Disperse the gloomy clouds of night
And death's dark shadows put to flight.
Rejoice! Rejoice! Emmanuel
Shall come to thee, O Israel.

O come, Thou Key of David, come,
And open wide our heavenly home;
Make safe the way that leads on high,
And close the path to misery.
Rejoice! Rejoice! Emmanuel
Shall come to thee, O Israel.

O come, O come, Thou Lord of might,
Who to Thy tribes, on Sinai's height,
In ancient times did'st give the Law,
In cloud, and majesty and awe.
Rejoice! Rejoice! Emmanuel
Shall come to thee, O Israel.

—Latin, 12th Century

A Mother's Prayer

....

Had I been Joseph's mother
I'd have prayed
protection from his brothers:
"God keep him safe;
he is so young,
so different from
the others."
Mercifully she never knew
there would be slavery
and prison, too.

Had I been Moses' mother
I'd have wept
to keep my little son;
praying she might forget
the babe drawn from the water
of the Nile,
had I not kept

him for her
nursing him the while?
Was he not mine
and she
but Pharaoh's daughter? . . .

Had I been Mary—
Oh, had I been she,
I would have cried
as never a mother cried,
". . . Anything, O God,
anything . . .
but crucified!"
With such prayers
importunate
my finite wisdom
would assail
Infinite Wisdom;
God, how fortunate
Infinite Wisdom
should prevail!

—Ruth Bell Graham's *Collected Poems*

To him who loves us and has freed
us from our sins by his blood,
and has made us to be a kingdom
and priests to serve his God
and Father—to him be glory and
power for ever and ever! Amen.

—REVELATION 1:5-6

CROWN

He Shall Reign Forever

T here's more to Christmas than the cradle and the Cross. There's also the crown. Chiseled into the cornerstone of the United Nations building is a quotation from the Bible that has never yet been fulfilled. Taken from Isaiah 2:4, it reads, "They shall beat their swords into plowshares and their spears into pruning hooks. Nation shall not lift up sword against nation, neither shall they learn war any more." This is a thrilling thought! It's often been repeated by men who long for peace. And many of those men wonder why peace doesn't come. However, this quotation must not be taken out of context.

The passage speaks of the time when the Messiah will reign over the whole earth. This is the era about which Jesus taught us to pray in the Lord's Prayer, "Thy Kingdom come,

Thy will be done in earth, as it is in heaven" (Matthew 6:10 KJV). This is the time when He who came as the baby of Bethlehem shall come back as King of kings and Lord of lords.

> The crown will not be restored until he to whom it rightfully belongs shall come; to him I will give it.
>
> —EZEKIEL 21:27

The kingdom of this world
Is become the kingdom of our Lord,
And of His Christ, and of His Christ;
And He shall reign for ever and ever.
King of kings, and Lord of lords, . . .
And He shall reign forever and ever,
King of kings, forever and ever,
And Lord of lords,
Hallelujah! Hallelujah!

—George Frideric Handel, *The Messiah*

For unto us a Child is born,
Unto us a Son is given;
And the government will be upon His
shoulder.
And His name will be called
Wonderful, Counselor, Mighty God,
Everlasting Father, Prince of Peace.
Of the increase of His government and
peace
There will be no end,
Upon the throne of David and over His
kingdom,
To order it and establish it with judg-
ment and justice
From that time forward, even forever.

—Isaiah 9:6–7 NKJV

The King of Kings

From His very birth, Christ was recognized as King. Something about Him inspired allegiance, loyalty, and homage. Wise men brought Him gifts. Shepherds fell down and worshipped Him. Herod, realizing that there is never room for two thrones in one kingdom, sought His life.

During His ministry, Jesus' claims upon people's lives were total and absolute. He allowed no divided loyalty. He demanded and received complete adoration and devotion. Mature men and women left their businesses and gave themselves in total obedience to Him. Many of them gave their lives, pouring out the last full measure of devotion.

Jesus' words caused even His most avowed enemies to say, "No man ever spoke like this Man!" (John 7:46 NKJV). And yet He was more than a poet, more than a statesman, more than a physician. We cannot understand Christ until we understand that He is the King of kings and the Lord of lords. Like Thomas, our response must be to bow down and confess, "My Lord and my God!" (John 20:28).

—*Hope for Each Day*

A scepter of righteousness is
the scepter of Your kingdom.

—PSALM 45:6 NKJV

A New Day Is Coming

This hope that was given to those shepherds on that first Christmas morning is available only to those who believe. To know the pardon, joy, peace, and power that come through Christ, we must personally receive Him by faith. We must humble ourselves and admit our sin and our moral failure. And then by faith we must turn to Him as Savior and Lord.

From two momentous events, the birth and death of Jesus, God says to us, "I love you." He also says, "I can forgive you."

Queen Victoria once heard a preacher preach on that subject. And she said, "I wish He would come in my lifetime, so I could lay my crown at His feet." Over one hundred fifty years ago, a French chemist named Pierre Bercheit said, "Within a hundred years of physical and chemical science, man will know what the atom is. It is my belief that when science reaches this stage, God will come down to earth with His big ring of keys and will say to humanity, 'Gentlemen, it is closing time.'" The Bible teaches that there will be a close to history as we know it. Man will have his last Armageddon. But when it seems that humanity is about to destroy itself, God will intervene. Christ will return.

> I looked, and there before me
>   was a white horse! Its rider
>   held a bow, and he was given
>   a crown, and he rode out as a
>   conqueror bent on conquest.

—REVELATION 6:2

O Holy Night

O holy night, the stars are brightly shining;
It is the night of the dear Savior's birth!
Long lay the world in sin and error pining,
Till He appeared and the soul felt its worth.
A thrill of hope, the weary soul rejoices,
For yonder breaks a new and glorious morn.
Fall on your knees, O hear the angel voices!
O night divine, O night when Christ was
    born!
O night, O holy night, O night divine!

Led by the light of faith serenely beaming,
With glowing hearts by His cradle we stand.
So led by light of a star sweetly gleaming,
Here came the wise men from Orient land.
The King of kings lay thus in lowly manger,
In all our trials born to be our Friend!

He knows our need—to our weakness is no
  stranger.
Behold your King; before Him lowly bend!
Behold your King; before Him lowly bend!

Truly He taught us to love one another;
His law is love and His Gospel is peace.
Chains shall He break for the slave is our
  brother
And in His Name all oppression shall
  cease.
Sweet hymns of joy in grateful chorus raise we,
Let all within us praise His holy Name!
Christ is the Lord! O praise His Name
  forever!
His pow'r and glory evermore proclaim!
His pow'r and glory evermore proclaim!

—Adolphe Charles Adam (1803–1856)
—John Sullivan Dwight (1813–1893)
—Placide Cappeau (1808–1877)

Holy Commander-in-Chief

....

A t the cradle, He was in the stall of an animal. At the Cross, He wore a crown of thorns. But when He comes again, it will be as commander-in-chief of the armies of Heaven. He will take control of this war-weary world and bring the permanent peace that we strive for and long for. A new world will be formed; a new social order will emerge. Many people wonder why it's taken so long, since He came over two thousand years ago, for all of this to be fulfilled. Why didn't He do it the first time? Well, something had to be done about our sins, so He died for our sins the first time. Why has it taken two thousand additional years of war and trouble and trials and difficulties and death and suffering and sorrow for this peace to come?

You remember in World War II there was D-Day? And then there was V-Day. And in between, there were many long months and thousands of casualties before the final victory was won.

The Cross was God's D-Day when the back of the enemy, namely sin and the devil, was broken. V-Day is when He returns in glory to set up His Kingdom.

In the intervening period, we have much work and much fighting to do. We must do our best to make His name known to all the world. We must do our best to keep the peace of the world. We must do our best to make better social conditions. The fact that we know that He is coming does not mean that we just sit on our haunches and sing hymns. He said, "Blessed is the servant who, when his master cometh, is found working."

Lay Them at His Feet

Lay them quietly at His feet one by one;
each desire, however sweet, just begun;
dreams still hazy, growing bright;
hope just poised, winged for flight;
all your longing, each delight—every one.
At His feet and leave them there,
never fear;
every heartache, crushing care—trembling
   tear;
you will find Him always true,
men may fail you, friends be few,
He will prove Himself to you
far more dear.

—Ruth Bell Graham's *Collected Poems*

For as lightning that comes
from the east is visible even
in the west, so will be the
coming of the Son of Man.

—MATTHEW 24:27

Fear Not

....

In the midst of the pessimism, gloom, and frustration of the present hour, we are not to wring our hands.

The angel said to the frightened shepherds, "Fear not" (Luke 2:10 KJV). Jesus says, "Fear not. I go and prepare a place for you and I will come again" (John 14:1–3).

The cradle, the Cross, and the crown are but three Acts in God's grand cosmic plan of the ages. Act I was that first Christmas when God entered history in a new way in Jesus Christ. In Act II, at the Cross, God solved the sin problem by Jesus Christ when He shed His blood for our sins. In Act III, which is yet to come, God will bring the world peace men yearn for—through Jesus Christ.

But we do see Jesus, who was made lower than the angels for a little while, now crowned with glory and honor because he suffered death, so that by the grace of God he might taste death for everyone.

—HEBREWS 2:9

Miracle Dreams

The mystic star dispensed its light,
A blind man moved about in sleep
And dreamed that he had sight.

"That night when shepherds heard the
    song
Of hosts angelic choiring near,
A deaf man moved in slumber's spell
And dreamed that he could hear.

"That night when in the cattle stall
Slept Child and mother, cheek by jowl,
A crippled moved his twisted limbs
And dreamed that he was whole.

"That night when o'er the newborn Babe
The tender Mary rose to lean,
A leper smiled in sleep
And dreamed that he was clean.

"That night when to the mother's breast
The little King was held secure,
A harlot slept a happy sleep
And dreamed that she was pure.

"That night when in the manger lay
The Sanctified who came to save,
A man moved in the sleep of death
And dreamed there was no grave."

—Susie M. Best

The Promise of Christmas

There is a popular song entitled "The King Is Coming." The King *is* coming and when He comes, sin will be eliminated. Tears will be wiped from every eye. Disease shall be no more and even death will be eliminated from the human scene. Nation shall not lift up sword against nation, and war shall be no more. This is the promise of Christmas. This is our hope. This is the Christmas star that lights our evening darkness. This is the assurance that a new day is coming, through the Messiah, whose name is called by Isaiah the prophet, "Wonderful Counselor, Mighty God, Everlasting Father, Prince of Peace" (Isaiah 9:6).

Christmas should be a time of renewed hope—not hope in the status quo, not hope in a particular concept, but hope in Jesus Christ. Hope that God is still in the shadow of history, hope that despite our tangled bungling, God will bring order out of chaos.

Today our imaginations go back two thousand years to that first Christmas when the world experienced three phenomena. First, there was a star. There were many stars in the sky, but none like this. This one shone with the aura and brilliance of another world. It was as though God had taken a lamp from the ceiling of heaven and hung it in the dark sky over a troubled world.

Second, there was a new song in the air. A world that had lost its song learned to sing again. With the coming of God in the flesh, hope sprang in the heart of man, and led by angelic beings, the whole world took up the refrain, "Glory to God in the highest, and on earth peace, good will toward men" (Luke 2:14 NKJV).

And third, there was good news—the good news that, at last, a Savior had come to save men from sin.

Jesus was the central theme of that first

Christmas. The star, the song, the gifts, the joy, the hope, the excitement—all were because of Him.

This is God's gift of Christmas:

- the cradle—His Son;
- the Cross—His life;
- the crown—His coming Kingdom.
  But . . . a gift, to be complete, must be received!

> Yet to all who did receive him,
> to those who believed in his
> name, he gave the right to
> become children of God.
>
> —JOHN 1:12